THE GIFT OF SPIRITUALITY

10 key principles *for* nurturing *the* soul

ROBERT F. MORNEAU

twentythirdpublications.com

TWENTY-THIRD PUBLICATIONS
A Division of Bayard
One Montauk Avenue, Suite 200
New London, CT 06320
(860) 437-3012 or (800) 321-0411
www.twentythirdpublications.com

Copyright ©2016 Robert F. Morneau. All rights reserved. No part of this publication may be reproduced in any manner without prior written permission of the publisher. Write to the Permissions Editor.

ISBN: 978-1-62785-152-7
Printed in the U.S.A.

Introduction

Everyone has a life of "the spirit," that is, awareness and consciousness of existence.

Spirituality means paying attention, with interior sensitivity to reality, aware that there is more to life than our personal philosophy. Spirituality connects us to God and makes us aware how that connectedness impacts our entire life.

How would you respond to the question, "How is your spiritual life going?" If a similar question were asked about our physical, social, intellectual, political, economic, or moral life, we might have a ready answer. But our spiritual life? We might be lost for words to share what is deep within our mind and heart.

One author said the nonspiritual life is being inattentive to Truth and Love. The spiritual life deals with living in the truth of things and responding with concern and compassion. At the heart of our spiritual life are Truth, Goodness, and Beauty. Not only are these graces available in various ways, but we are called to be agents of Truth, Goodness, and Beauty. This mutual receiving and transmitting of them is at the core of a spiritual life.

The daily demands of making a living, raising a family, nurturing friendship, seeking employment, dealing with health issues, or dealing with past hurts and traumas can distract us from living deeply. Perhaps they are perceived as not being part of spirituality. The challenge is integration. Then, throw in economic crises, political strife, technological bombardment, and radical secularism, and we realize how difficult it is to have a Center in which to live. These many facets make it difficult to discern our calling, our vocation as agents of God's grace.

Nevertheless, God's Spirit sustains and surrounds us. We live in a "divine milieu," and we need but keep our eyes and ears open to see and hear God's abiding grace. Perhaps our "everyday spirituality" comes down to what the Carmelite religious St. Thérèse of Lisieux calls "the little way," doing everything with love. Be it laundry, mowing the lawn, taking out the garbage, changing diapers, driving to work, writing a letter, making a phone call—we grow toward spiritual maturity by doing it all with love.

#1 PPP Principle:
*Spirituality is about **perspective**, **proportion**, and **pacing**.*[1]

Absolutizing is a great danger, that is, allowing the part to become the whole. Too easily we identify with one particular negative, death-dealing trait even to the exclusion of the positive and life-giving graced moments.

The Carmelite poet Jessica Powers captures powerfully this tendency to absolutize in her poem "The Tear in the Shade:"[2]

The Tear in the Shade

I tore the new pale window shade with slightly
more than a half-inch tear.
I knew the Lady would be shocked to see
what I had done with such finality.

I went outside to lose my worry there.
Later when I came back into the room
it seemed that nothing but the tear was there.

There had been furniture, a rug, and pictures,
and on the table flowers in purple boom.
It was amazing how they dwindled, dwindled,
and how the tear grew till it filled the room.

Proportion is a vital element in a healthy spirituality. It requires moderation, avoiding extremes. The challenge is to give sufficient time and energy to the four demands in everyone's life: worship, work, love, and leisure. If any of the four demands leads to the exclusion of the other three, our spiritual life will suffer—as often will the lives of those around us, because spirituality has a social dimension.

Balance is another name for proportion. The volume of activities and multiple opportunities for various endeavors increasingly threatens a balanced life. Even the principle of "putting first things first" (priority) becomes a challenge. What really is the most important value? We need to constantly assess where we put our energy and time to maintain proportion.

There is also the question of pacing: "too fast, too slow." Hurriedness threatens the quality of life. Pope Francis coined the word "rapidification" to describe this hurriedness. We get "through experiences" but get little "from experiences" when we rush. We wake up one morning and realize that life is passing us by.

A dangerous partner to hurriedness is procrastination, putting things off. It is not going "too slow," but going nowhere. "Get going!" the Spirit whispers/shouts to us: get going in helping the needy, asking forgiveness, doing quality work. Turtles have the prerogative of moving slowly; we humans do not. We have to move out of the starting blocks to find a proper pace to live in the Holy Spirit.

#2 Developmental Principle:
Spirituality is about growing into the person God wants us to be.

Is there a way to assess one's spiritual life? Evelyn Underhill (1875–1941) studied the mystics and saints. According to her study, six characteristics of spirituality are fundamental to spiritual development.[3]

Self-surrender! In Gethsemane and in the Annunciation story, we "see" self-surrender. Jesus, in great anguish, put the Father's will above his own; Mary, in her fear and unknowing, asked that God's will be done, whatever the price. A major struggle is to discern God's will in our unique circumstances. Once discerned, we need the grace to say: "Your will, not mine, be done." This is self-surrender.

Silence! Silence involves an inner quietude that enables us to hear the whispers (and shouts) of God. To sit quietly and wait upon the voice of God is a spiritual exercise of immense importance. God longs to speak to our heart; our soul longs to hear the message of love and mercy.

Leisure! Leisure is as much an attitude as it is having downtime. We take a break from our duties and seek some refreshment, perhaps redirection. This is not "wasting time"; it is similar to a fallow field. It is a time of renewal and replenishing. Leisure is not a luxury; it is a spiritual necessity.

Faithfulness! Making promises is at the heart of our human journey. "I promise to be true to you...." Such commitments put us into meaningful and stable relationships with God and others. Infidelity wreaks havoc on our personal life and social order. Spirituality is about keeping one's word. Our faithfulness is a response to the fidelity of God, who calls us to covenant, a deep, abiding, love relationship.

Kindness! St. Paul lists kindness as one of the nine signs of the Holy Spirit's presence. Kindnesses—a pat on the back, a word of encouragement, a note of gratitude, a phone call—express love, our concern for others. The spiritual life is a series of kindnesses, even when expressed as tough love.

Courage! Confronting suffering and death, the rejection of others and loss of employment, the guilt of our conscience and fears of our heart—what courage is needed! St. Paul exemplified the courage of a disciple as he proclaimed the message of Jesus despite being stoned, beaten, and experiencing misfortunes at every turn. Individuals who confront racial injustice, discrimination, and oppression of any sort witness courage. We do well to pray daily that the Holy Spirit will pour out the grace of courage into our frightened hearts.

Again, Evelyn Underhill says it well: "First let us speak of courage, pluck, real love of the hard to do, a willingness to take risks, to face difficult problems, to suffer, to persevere at whatever cost, to find initiative and zest in overcoming human reluctance, and to accept the austere side of our Christian profession, the fact that it makes absolute demands on us."[4]

#3 Mercy Principle:
Spirituality is about living the gospel's game-plan.

The first cousin of mercy is compassion. In the Gospel of Matthew we read: "At the sight of crowds, [Jesus'] heart was moved with pity for them because they were troubled and abandoned, like sheep without a shepherd" (9:36). There is no way of understanding the life of Jesus without realizing that his heart constantly ached at the sight of suffering, be it physical, psychological, or spiritual. His was also a heart of mercy. Time and again he brought healing and consolation to the lonely and deeply troubled.

Spirituality is grounded in compassion and mercy. One's spiritual life is authentic to the extent it finds expression in serving those in need—the hungry and thirsty, the homeless and imprisoned, the sick and discouraged. More, the spiritual life demands that we forgive injuries and embrace wrongs patiently, console the grieving and bring knowledge to the ignorant, invite the lost into the circle of God's light, and counsel the lonely. What a demanding and joyful life.

Two pictures of mercy merit our contemplation. First, the prodigal son (Luke 15:11–32). Rembrandt's famous painting depicts an aged, frail father embracing his wayward son. Such is our merciful God; such are we to be. The second image (Matthew 18:21–35) is of the man who asked forgiveness of a huge debt and then, within the hour, refused mercy to someone indebted to him. For many, the story hits home.

Mercy, compassion, and forgiveness are cornerstones of spirituality.

Suggestion: use the corporal and spiritual works of mercy as a game plan for life. Every week, put one into action. One week, visit someone in jail, either in person or by writing; one week, get to the hospital or nursing home; another week, pray in a special way for those who have died. With practical flexibility, make an intentional act of doing the gospel imperatives. Such specificity witnesses to how seriously we take our vocation as disciples of the Lord.

#4 Authenticity Principle:
Spirituality is about authentic holiness.

As Eliza sings in *My Fair Lady*, "Don't talk of stars burning above; if you're in love, show me!" This captures well our spiritual journey. The spoken word demands little energy; the loving deed demands sacrifice. We are speaking of a committed, consecrated life, the life given to us in baptism. At the core is self-giving that, as with Jesus and many saints, leads to suffering and death. Thomas Green, SJ, reminds us that "any spirituality which neglects the demands of fraternal love and concern—even the demands of love of one's enemies—cannot be authentically Christian."[5]

A faith-filled life means refusing to allow complexity to dominate us. The choice to focus on essentials and not peripheral things is a mature freedom. Further, our faith calls us to be prayerful and loving toward all. Here are the two poles of spirituality: adoration and service, prayer and reaching out. No one can claim to be a person of faith without obeying God's will. This alignment brings peace. Humility means living truth; detachment means traveling light and being missionary in nature. We give evidence of our spirituality and faith life by suffering and sacrifice. In dying to our false self and living in God's image, we prove ourselves daughters and sons of a loving, merciful God.

Often our lives are without success (vain) and unproductive (sterile). Emily Dickinson wrote a poem arguing that if we can stop one heart from breaking or help one bird back into its nest, we shall not live in vain. Simple acts of kindness, done in the atmosphere of eternity, have eternal consequences. The difficult parable about the barren fig tree shows that although surrounded by the grace of friendship and good education, our lives can still be sterile without self-giving. God and the world expect much. Only as good stewards of God's gifts will we convince the world of the beauty of the spiritual life.

Dorothy Day (1897-1980), cofounder of the Catholic Worker Movement, gave witness by her commitment to the poor and suffering. But she had to struggle with inner demons. She wrote: "I had an ugly sense of the futility of human effort, man's helpless misery, the triumph of might." Her powerful memoir, *The Long Loneliness*, traces her transformation by God's grace. She became a significant witness of a gospel life, despite her sins and failings. Her life was not in vain or sterile.

#5 AAA Principle:
*Spirituality is about a life of **attention**, **adherence**, and **abandonment**.*

Douglas Steere (1901-95), a Quaker whose philosophy and social service touched thousands, consistently spoke about three dimensions of a fully human and Christian life. These were *attention* to the ever-present love of God; *adherence* to those gospel values and attitudes that have priority in our life; and *abandonment* to God's will as revealed in our unique lives. For Steere, there was a cognitive, affective, and behavioral element to our spiritual life.

Attention! To be truly present to a flower in the crannied wall or a windhover in the sky or the pudgy nose of a newborn babe is no small feat. Tennyson and Hopkins and grandmothers are attentive. They notice things; they appreciate beauty and the grandeur of God. The challenge is focus and a willingness to embrace limitations. We cannot be conscious of everything. In choosing to be aware of the person in front of us, we have to let go of the crowd around us, however momentarily. In choosing to turn to God in contemplative prayer, we set aside interesting spiritual reading and even the Bible. Attention is a discipline of the highest order.

Adherence! The heart is a symbol of desire and passion. Not only do we come to know ourselves (and others) by what we pay attention to, we also know them by discovering what gains entrance into the human heart. It is possible to adhere to possessions and power, to prestige and pleasure. But it is also possible to cling to God.

Abandonment! To watch a child leap off a ledge into dad's waiting arms is to witness abandonment. To watch passengers parade into a jumbo jet for an international flight is to witness abandonment. To watch Thomas Merton enter the Trappist monastery in Gethsemani, Kentucky, is to witness abandonment.

The exercise of freedom is amazing. Individuals who live a committed life (e.g., Dorothy Day or Dag Hammarskjöld or Gandhi) exemplify the essence of the spiritual life: service. It is all about being *for* others; about transcending our narrow individualistic lives, abandoning ourselves to a noble purpose—one that fosters life and unity. In David Brooks' excellent work *The Road to Character*,[6] he said that for Dorothy Day, sin was separation, and holiness was unity. Day expressed spiritual abandonment by living with the poor in costly solidarity. We desperately need models (and mentors) of abandonment.

#6 "True Self" Principle:
Spirituality is about living out of the center of our true self and relating to the "true" God revealed in Jesus.

Thomas Merton wrote extensively about the struggle between our true and false self. Self-knowledge is difficult. Too easily we identity our self with our role in society, what others think of us, and what we think of our self. The true self is buried under false images. A central spiritual goal is to grow in our understanding of who (and whose) we are. Appropriating the reality that we are made to God's image and likeness may take years.

To complicate the matter, idolatry reigns. Spirituality deals with our relationship with God and how that relationship impacts our lives. But who is God? What is our theology? What is our image of the Deity? We often misunderstand the mystery of God. Given our limited intelligence and often weak faith, it is no surprise that our struggle to relate to God is so intense.

Images impact our attitudes and behavior. For some, the self is a struggling pilgrim or an entrusted gardener or a beloved daughter or son. For others, the self is an accidental tourist or an "immortal diamond" or a wounded healer. Maybe we are all of these on different days and in different seasons. Self-knowledge is a lifelong work.

And our image of God? Jesus presents his Father as a God of love, forgiveness, and compassion, demanding our total consecration. Some see God as a severe judge, a distant force, or a figment of human imagination. Spirituality's cornerstone is the mystery of a gracious and loving God.

I am indebted to George Herbert, the seventeenth-century Anglican priest and poet, for giving me in nine lines an image (theology) of God that is profound and biblically accurate. God is at once creator, redeemer, sanctifier, healer, and enricher. To put this poem to heart is to rearrange the furniture of our soul:

Trinitie Sunday

> Lord, who hast form'd me out of mud,
> > And hast redeem'd me through thy bloud,
> > And sanctifi'd me to do good;
>
> Purge all my sinnes done heretofore:
> > For I confess my heavie score,
> > And I will strive to sinne no more.
>
> Enrich my heart, mouth, hands in me,
> > With faith, with hope, with charitie;
> > That I may runne, rise, rest with thee.[7]

#7 LLL Principle:
*Spirituality is about receiving God's **light**, **love**, and **life** and sharing those graces with others.*

When the Carmelite religious Blessed Elizabeth of the Trinity (1880-1906) was dying, her last words were "I am going to Light, to Life, to Love!" A fifth-century Sufi prayer has this petition: "Accept, O gracious God, this my emptiness, and so fill me with Thyself, Thy light, Thy love, Thy life…" In the Liturgy of the Hours, this line appears: "Turn our thoughts to what is holy and may we ever live in the light of your love" (III, p. 926). Our God is a God of Light (1 John 1:5), a God of Love (1 John 4:16), and a God of Life (John 14:6). As creatures made in God's image and likeness, we are to be open to these graces and pass them on to all we meet.

Light! There is darkness in the world; there is darkness in each of us. True, there is a holy darkness described powerfully in Barbara Brown Taylor's *Learning to Walk in the Dark*.[8] And in John of the Cross, we hear about the dark night of the soul and how God's presence needs discernment. But in the end, we are made to see, and we are made for light, a light that reveals truth. Revelation is about seeing epiphanies. Our baptismal call includes becoming an agent of light.

Love! The great mysteries of our faith—creation, redemption, sanctification—express divine Love. The God revealed in Jesus cares passionately for all creation. It is an authentic love because of presence. God so loved the world as to become one of us in the Incarnation. No deistic god here who makes and abandons his work. Rather, like a faithful parent, God creates and abides with us still. That Love summons us to show concern and compassion to all we meet.

Life! Julius Caesar supposedly said: "Veni, vidi, vici" ("I came, I saw, I conquered"). Jesus, if we listen carefully, might have said: "Veni, vidi, amavi" ("I came, I saw, I loved"). We know Jesus came to bring life (John 10:10). More, he came to bring life to the full. The gift of the Eucharist offers us God's life and love in a unique way. This sacrifice and meal nourish and refresh. In this banquet of love, we are called to become missionary disciples caught up in the wonderful ministry of receiving and giving life. The vocation of becoming life-givers is at the center of our baptismal call.

#8 Spirituality Components Principle:
*Spirituality is characterized by **presence**, dialogue, and **solitude**.*[9]

"Always there and seldom noticed" is a phrase Evelyn Underhill used to lament our lack of awareness of God's holy presence. The gift of faith assures us of the abiding, ubiquitous presence of God. To live with the realization that Love surrounds and sustains us is a grace beyond description. To be certain of God's presence changes everything and calls us to share that experience with others by reflecting God's glory in a life of service.

The quality of a relationship is proportionate to the quality of communication. At the core of spirituality is the dialogue between God and an individual (and community). This conversation, be it through Scripture, Tradition, or stirrings of the heart, deepens and expands the relationship. If dialogue is not sustained, friendships weaken and sometimes are abandoned. Dialogue between the soul and God is essential.

It would seem that solitude removes one from others, if not from God. But there is a holy solitude, a graced silence. Thomas Merton maintained that when he went to the hermitage in the woods, he was never closer to this community, though the monastery was some distance away. Paradoxically, distance can promote nearness. Physical separation does not preclude spiritual oneness. Such is our relationship with God through solitude.

#9 The Expansion / Contraction Principle: *Grace causes the soul to expand; sin causes contraction.*[10]

St. Thérèse of Lisieux's autobiography, *The Story of a Soul,* reveals someone attuned to the slightest expansion or contraction of her heart and soul. Love expands, sin contracts; certain places expand, others contract; certain individuals open us to new life, others cause us to become narrow and confined. Listen to St. Thérèse's firsthand experience:

> He [Therese's father] took us to the convent and there I experienced a sort of *contraction of my heart* such as I never felt at the sight of the monastery. This monastery produced the opposite effect which Carmel produced in me, for there everything made my heart expand (92); Each evening I was back home, fortunately, and then my heart expanded (53); I felt my soul expand... (173); I felt my heart contract... (179); It is only charity that can expand my heart... (226); I can see with joy that in loving Him the heart expands... (237).[11]

Smiles expand our hearts; frowns contract them. Affirmations enlarge our lives; words of negation narrow them. Affability (and risibility) opens our hearts; hostility (and sadness) closes them. Here are grace and sin, energies that give life and bring death. This is the land of light and darkness, wherein light enables us to see and darkness precludes vision. The spiritual life is in constant flux, expanding and contracting, depending upon events and circumstances.

Part of our baptismal commitment is to be expanders, not contractors. In calling us to fullness of life, Jesus commands us to love one another. Love and charity expand, enlarge, and enrich our lives. Apathy and indifference contract, narrow, and impoverish us. Perhaps another translation of Moses' choice to his people was expansion or contraction, besides life or death.

#10 The Human Imperfection Principle: *Spirituality embraces imperfection as an essential element.*[12]

Saint Paul had that mysterious thorn in the flesh; Augustine struggled with concupiscence; Mother Teresa of Calcutta wrote about frequent doubts and fears. These fellow pilgrims confirm that no one is exempt from the dark elements of our spiritual journey. Yet in these Achilles tendons, God's power can operate in unique and surprising ways.

Time and time again we hear about an illness (of body or mind) bringing a reexamination of one's life, how job loss and a sense of failure turn out to be a blessing, or how sin might throw one into the merciful arms of God. It is true that illness, loss, sin can destroy. Yet they can also be avenues of grace and salvation.

Pride and perfectionism are dead ends. Pride is as much stupidity as a sin; perfectionism, the real impossible dream, cannot be achieved on Earth. What can point us in the direction of God's redemptive love is a humble heart and contrite spirit. Through the Holy Spirit and grace of spiritual sensibility and sensitivity, we can both discern God's will and receive the courage to respond to whatever the Lord asks of us.

SPIRITUAL EXERCISES

1] Give thanks!

At the end of the day, jot down one way you have been blessed or gifted: a good meal, a beautiful sunset, a letter from a friend, an unexpected compliment. Pause and offer thanks. Then jot down one way you blessed or gifted someone: a pat on the back, a smile, careful listening, a word of affirmation. Reflect upon your generosity. The spiritual life is deeply enriched by gratitude (not taking anything for granted) and consistently being thoughtful.

2] Examine your Consciousness

Back in 1972, Father George Aschenbrenner, SJ, wrote an article on the Ignatian practice of examining our inner movements and noting our response (or lack of response) to them. God constantly nudges, prods, whispers, and calls everyone to a life of love. The old "examination of conscience" focused on assessing if actions were good or not. This examination of *consciousness* goes deeper and looks to life's inner movements. We do well to pause and, after invoking the help of the Holy Spirit, review our day in God's loving presence at this deeper level.

3] Practice living in the presence of God

Edith Stein (St. Teresa Benedicta of the Cross, 1891–1942) begins a prayer: "God is here in these moments and can give us in a single instant exactly what we need." Henri Nouwen writes in *The Genesse Diary*: "To live a spiritual life is to live in the presence of God."[13] The spiritual life seeks to live consciously in God's all-embracing love and mercy. Our challenge is not to forget the mystery of God's abiding presence.

4] Pay attention to detail

Just as carpenters have a tool box, all humans need a spiritual tool box. One tool is attention, a consistent mindfulness of our daily experience. That attention is not limited to large issues. Mindfulness is also directed to the little things: what to eat, smiling at a stranger, expressing gratitude for a compliment, and the list goes on.

Failure to be present to details often leads to failure to be aware of larger matters. If the devil is in the details, so is grace. Aelred Squire writes: "God uses little, bright, sharp, vivid things to teach us incomprehensible things."[14] A needle, a spade, a wildflower offer their own small epiphany—*if* we are attentive.

5] Yield to the promptings of love and truth

Pope Francis, in his encyclical *Laudato Si'*, stresses the importance of attentiveness: "We are speaking of an attitude of the heart, one which approaches life with serene attentiveness, which is capable of being fully present to someone without thinking of what comes next, which accepts each moment as a gift from God to be lived to the full."[15]

This living in the "sacrament of the moment" is a rich part of Christian tradition. Because of the fast pace of life and multiple stimuli, it is difficult to remain focused. Thus, the stirrings of love slip past us, and the epiphanies of truth go unnoticed. We desperately need the grace of sensitivity and sensibility as well as the courage to respond to God's proddings.

6] Foster a mellow soul
Gustavo Gutierrez, the South American theologian, wrote about the need to keep our soul mellow and grateful. He stressed the importance of friendship and creativity, of healthy leisure and a glass of wine. Sage advice. Too easily we can become hard instead of mellow, ungrateful instead of eucharistic.

A beautiful prayer in the Liturgy of the Hours might help us foster a mellow heart:
> Lord, teach us goodness, discipline and wisdom
> and these gifts will keep us from becoming
> hardened by evil,
> weakened by laziness,
> and ignorant because of foolishness.

7] Name grace
In the garden of Eden, Adam had the task of naming his fellow creatures. A mighty task it was. We have the task of naming the gifts of divine life and love we encounter as well as the sins that injure and rupture relationships. Naming means we have some understanding of life and some degree of self-knowledge.

St. Paul is a master namer! His letter to the Galatians (5:19–23) gives a rich vocabulary. Sins: anger, quarrels, fornication, impurity, idolatry, sorcery, strife, enmities, dissensions, factions, carousing, drunkenness, jealousy, envy. Graces: gentleness, self-control, patience, kindness, love, joy, faithfulness, peace.

Each day we are invited to name what gives life and what takes life. A worthy (and necessary) endeavor it is.

NOTES

1. Joseph Gallagher, *How to Survive Being Human* (Westminster: Christian Classics, Inc., 1970), p. 137.

2. *Selected Poetry of Jessica Powers*, ed. By Regina Siegfried, ASC and Robert F. Morneau (Kansas City: Sheed & Ward, 1989), p. 118. Used with permission.

3. Dana Greene, *Evelyn Underhill: Artist of the Infinite Life* (NY: Crossroad, 1990), p. 75.

4. Evelyn Underhill, *The Ways of the Spirit* (NY: Crossroad, 1993), p. 155.

5. Thomas Greene, *When the Well Runs Dry* (South Bend, IN: Ave Maria Press, 2007), p. 63.

6. David Brooks, *The Road to Character* (NY: Random House, 2015).

7. George Herbert, "Trinitie Sunday," *The Temple* (1633).

8. Barbara Brown Taylor, *Learning to Walk in the Dark* (San Francisco: HarperOne, 2014).

9. Francois Roustang, SJ, *Growth in the Spirit*, trans. by Kathleen Pond (NY: Sheed and Ward, 1966), p. 39.

10. Evelyn Underhill, *The House of the Soul & Concerning the Inner Life* (Minneapolis, MN: The Seabury Press, 1947), p. 103.

11. *Story of a Soul: The Autobiography of St. Thérèse of Lisieux*, trans. John Clarke, O.C.D. (Washington, DC: ICS Publications, 1975).

12. Thomas Moore, *Care of the Soul* (NY: Harper Collins Publishers, 1992), pp. 262-263.

13. Henri J. M. Nouwen, *The Genesse Diary: Report from a Trappist Monastery* (NY: Doubleday & Company, Inc., 1976), p. 152.

14. Aelred Squire, *Asking the Fathers* (Westminster, MD: Christian Classics, 1973), p. 98.

15. Pope Francis, *Laudato Si'* (Rome: Libreria Editrice Vaticana, 2015), no. 226.